WINGSPAN

Talent Management -
Gaining Corporate Dominance

ADRIENNE M. SOMERVILLE

authorHOUSE®

AuthorHouse™
1663 Liberty Drive
Bloomington, IN 47403
www.authorhouse.com
Phone: 833-262-8899

Published by AuthorHouse 03/18/2021

ISBN: 978-1-6655-1848-2 (sc)
ISBN: 978-1-6655-1847-5 (hc)
ISBN: 978-1-6655-1850-5 (e)

Print information available on the last page.

This book is printed on acid-free paper.

Have you ever walked into a room, introduced yourself, discussed a topic, and had no idea where the conversation would take you in minutes—dare I say years? In 2008, when I met Michele (Mickey) DeMoss-Coward, I had no idea our professional meeting and talent management discussion would result in a friendship of a lifetime, as well as the manifestation of this literary work. Our casual, professional introduction inspired me to mature my interests in talent management while motivating me to share my learned knowledge, demonstrated experience, and proven results with you.

I would like to take full credit for independently capitalizing on this book concept, but I know had it not been for the consistent support of my accountability partner, it may have taken me years, if ever, to complete this book. I could consume the space of this entire book with accolades and praises for always being my champion, coach, confidant, friend, and fellow talent management subject matter expert.

Moreover, I want to offer you what she offered me, which is consistent encouragement to discover your talents, and more importantly, the inspiration to enable the talents of others. While reading this book, it is my sincerest hope you connect with someone you admire, appreciate, and love dearly, someone you would want to dedicate your first literary piece to.

Mickey, you amazingly *rock*, you "Power Puff" girl! Thank you for being the blessing you are to all whom you have encountered. You are a talent management difference maker along this journey of *transforming organizations one person at a time.*

CONTENTS

CONTENTS

PREFACE

Chapter 1 defines talent management and shares four fundamental talent management principles. These four talent management principles are understanding your products and services; documenting required skills and experiences; identifying the talent across the organization and performing gap analysis, and lastly infusing risk mitigation strategies and resources that enable career development and management. The aforementioned four principles are critical to the success of applying talent management throughout any organization.

Chapter 2 provides a guided list of talent management questions to enable and facilitate talent management discussions across organizations. The purpose of this chapter is to support the goal of creating an organizational culture that applies, understands and embraces talent management, at all levels.

Chapter 3 identifies supportive talent management attributes and characteristics that will ensure you achieve your talent management goals. Specifically, in this chapter, you will learn more about a checklist of helpful hints to assist you along your talent management journey.

Chapter 4 shares the importance of understanding the product and service lines based on organizational work demands. Specifically, what does your company offer, and how do people in the organization deliver products and services? The focus is not on what your workforce members do but what your workforce members should be doing. Are they clear on what they should be doing in support of the organization?

Chapter 5 examines the second principle of talent management, documenting required skills and experiences. This includes the value of transparency and empowerment associated with sharing the most critical aspects regarding the required knowledge, skills and abilities (KSAs) across all technical and leadership behavioral competencies, spanning various levels of proficiency within an organization.

Chapter 6 discusses the third principle of talent management and shifts to identify the talent across your organization by performing gap assessments and analysis. This chapter is about understanding the power of self-assessing and the ability to perform true self- assessments while providing feedback on the assessments of others. At the conclusion of this chapter, you will understand how to manifest talent gaps into positions of power and opportunity when you understand your gaps and embrace constructive feedback.

Chapter 7 focuses on the talent management principle centered on how to infuse risk mitigation strategies and resources that enable career development and management. At the conclusion of this chapter you will understand how to address the principles of talent management and their tie to an organizational action plan that serves as a demand signal for human resource activities, focused on maximizing talent management, optimizing performance, and building profits.

Chapter 8 discusses the various types of mentorship. In addition, I provide insight into the benefits of mentoring that encompass the mentor and protégé, identifying individual, managerial, and organizational gains.

Chapter 9 includes several interview responses that offer talent management experiences and personal stories, from a range of professionals who have consistently applied and witnessed the benefits of talent management and its implications. Although not commonly known, much like unsung heroes, these professionals in government, industry, and nonprofit organizations have increased the production, performance, and profits of their organizations with the application of talent management principles.

Lastly, after reading Chapter 10, you will feel confident that you too can leverage the value of talent management in support of your organization's mission and goals.

INTRODUCTION

TALENT MANAGEMENT MATTERS

When I initially began to write this book, the concept of information was solely centered on talent management. A renewed calling for organizations to improve their production, performance and profits by focusing on the development and management of their people, from the inside out, was my initial thought. However, it occurred to me that what we need most is for leaders to improve leveraging the talents of all people, at all levels, within their organizations. The capitalization of talent within an organization has proven, for decades, to be the best vantage point for the most successful leaders.

Moreover, many books have been written about talent management, the workforce dynamic, a workforce that operates as one, and career development and management; yet there are still organizations attempting to operate with the wrong people in the wrong positions at the wrong time. Interestingly, many of these organizations often question their inability to achieve objectives and increase profits, despite their aggressive investments in talent acquisition. Today's challenge in talent management is often represented by individual leaders inconsistently attempting to perform workforce planning by, for example, identifying work requirements, analyzing the existing workforce, equating skills gaps to staffing gaps, or relying on adding new resources to rectify workforce weaknesses. These efforts are ineffectual, often lacking any consistent standards or a cohesive long-term talent management strategy.

For years we have seen in the value, mission, and vision statements of many organizations the words "people first." Yet when you have a conversation with the average employee, he or she often does not feel as if he or she is first at all. Today, I offer the establishment of a new standard of ensuring employees, at all levels, know they represent the organization's most valuable resource: its talent! In essence, people are the bedrock of all organizations, upon which talent management and all other company enablers rests.

You might ask, "How will I know if my organization is truly performing talent management? Are our talent management efforts visible to every employee?"

First, ask yourself if your organization has the ability to align people's leadership and technical talent with mission, strategy, and product delivery. Also, is your organization able to identify specific competencies (analytical, technical, education, and experience) to cultivate for continued organizational growth?

Hopefully, you responded, "I intend to read this book to apply the best industry practices to influence my organization by introducing new talent management activities." Despite your responses, at this point you should feel good because you are taking positive steps to lead your organization down the right talent management path, regardless of its talent management position today.

Additionally, I want to share the top talent management concepts with interested readers like you, because I believe you will not only read this book but will take the necessary action to spearhead your organization's talent management initiatives company-wide. So how do you do this in an organization, this whole talent management thing? How does talent management happen in most organizations?

When meeting with different leaders, they often confide their lack of understanding of talent management. I recommend you do not focus on what you have done wrong or what aspects of talent management you have not gotten right. This book is about learning, applying, and improving, so you are able to advance your talent management agenda. In addition, this book is about pivoting, if need be, and course correcting accordingly to establish and achieve your talent management goals and objectives.

I also want to convey the need to not only understand talent management but the data and its organizational value. We must learn the importance of collecting data about our workforce, since it is the foundation regarding the knowledge, skills and abilities of workforce members. Whether this is your first talent management read or you are a seasoned professional, you will find keys to help you design, develop, and deploy a rewarding and successful talent management program.

Finally, at the conclusion of this book, you will learn how to apply talent management principles and processes to enable productive progress that builds strong performance and profits. I hope your takeaways are good insight and a strong impulse that urge you to take immediate action within your organization now that you are fully aware of exactly why talent management matters and the significance of its successful organizational contributions.

1

DEFINING TALENT MANAGEMENT

Does your company level up its use of talent management, making decisions based on direct responses provided by each workforce member, or does your company simply leverage generic data about its workforce, typically provided by its technical or Human Resource managers, to make decisions? What is the talent management approach of your company? Specifically, does your organization lack a consistent and standard approach to capture information, such as policies, processes, and tools to identify talent and assess skill gap areas, accurately managing and anticipating staffing, and mitigating potential personnel and program risk?

Companies make significant investments in hiring people and attempting to retain them by investing in training and other career-development programs. I have noticed in many instances when there is a much-needed talent management discussion, people immediately digress, pivoting from the talent management discussion to having a human resource, human strategies, or human capital discussion. Although I understand the application of human capital to human resources was to add value to people within an organization, it is worth noting the commonly used human capital reference, for some people, elicits a negative connotation. The reference to people as valuable assets, in lieu of just commodities, is really the intent of the words human capital.

Talent management is often confused with human resources, human strategies, or human capital. While independent, talent management and human resources are interdependent. Specifically, talent management represents the organizational activities that generate the demand signal for human resources to hire or train. Simply stated, the results of talent management activities are the basis upon which all other workforce decisions should reply. Talent management is the catalyst for Human Resource activities. So how do they interdependently operate?

First and foremost, talent management is the critically important identification and analysis of the required knowledge, skills and abilities (KSAs) the organization needs to effectively and efficiently deliver its products and services. Talent management is the comprehensive identification, at a granular level, of the capabilities of the workforce—their skills, products, and competencies—not in what they do in their current position but in their entire talent portfolio. Talent management also provides the organization the data to determine exactly where there is a skill gap between the KSAs required by the organization and those possessed by the current workforce.

The interdependence between talent management and human resources is the result of identifying the skills gaps of the current workforce. Leadership determines the most effective methods to close the identified gaps. Does hiring represent the best method to overcome that deficiency, or does the data direct leadership to recognize that a significant number of the current workforce lack those KSAs, and training would be the most effective method to close that gap? Leadership communicates the resulting action to the workforce. Talent management is the conduit that allows the organization to make targeted decisions with confidence.

Supervisors and managers play a more intimate role in talent management than human resources by analyzing the outcomes of the employees' assessments, identifying perceived gaps in the required skill sets at every level, and gaining insight to mitigate personnel and project risks. In order to establish a corrective action plan, insight and understanding of the following questions are critical:

1. Do a significant number of employees lack the required knowledge, skills, or abilities?
2. Does existing training provide the knowledge required to perform work functions?
3. Are today's training investments aligned to meet today's training demands?
4. Would cross-training allow an employee to increase essential skills and improve abilities?
5. Are some training offerings less relevant because they focused on obsolete skills?
6. Is advanced training or hiring the better course of action?

Once managers and leaders have determined whether the company's new training courses or hiring activities represent the most effective course of action, it is then that Human Resources become involved in the talent management solution process implementation. The actions taken in the world of Human Resources are based on the findings from talent management.

Allow me to further highlight the differences in organizational activities between talent management and human resources by providing additional examples of talent management initiatives, such as vacancy/need specification and identification; documentation and development of relevant leadership and technical training; career path mapping; progress to plan goal setting, mentoring, and coaching;

succession planning and organization assessment; and statistical analysis of knowledge and skill-gap impacts. Depending on the organization, these talent management initiatives may occur in one such department or as embedded functions in many larger departments.

Talent management is the heart of every optimally performing organization. The words talent management are often misconstrued and misused. Talent management is a conscious and deliberate approach to attract, engage, develop, retain, and reward people with the aptitude and abilities to meet current and future organizational needs. Another way of viewing talent management is the strategic manner in which you are able to align and manage the right resources across the organization to deliver the right products at the right time, which includes the right talent teams.

The term talent management is defined as the connection between human resource development and organizational effectiveness. This term has been realized since the 1970s, where many high-performing companies that survived economic shifts recognized that identifying, quantifying, and leveraging the talent of its people provides a competitive advantage. Following a 1997 study, management consulting company McKinsey & Company introduced the term "talent management." They stated the way to win with talent is knowing that people, not companies, generate value. Companies such as Booz Allen Hamilton, Deloitte, and IBM are among the many that also embraced talent management and are reaping the benefits. Talent management is systematic, data-driven, and quantifiable. It leverages the as-is state of the workforce and its attributes and allows us to anticipate and predict the to-be state of the workforce. In addition, talent management continues to be extremely valuable at the individual, managerial, and organizational levels.

Talent management is a strategic way in which we approach people, not only from a leadership or managerial perspective but from a valued-person perspective. Talent management is the ability to close not just a staffing gap that is a Human Resources function. It also closes a *skill* gap within an organization that safeguards optimal performance. In addition, it is an underpinning of an organization's perspective of its people. Talent management may be performed for its employees within existing departments or by leadership across multiple departments to accurately identify and assess the knowledge, skills and abilities required to create new departments and generate current and future hiring actions.

For example, the talent management process identifies how many people, with the required skills, reside within a department or division. It also confirms if the right skills needed are available and accessible within an organization or beyond. If the right skills are not available at the right time, talent management generates a hiring or training demand signal. The training demand warrants leaders consider the relevance of the current training offerings and future training investments. If the current training is not focused on closing the skill gaps, as training serves as an organizational risk mitigation strategy, then the need to identify targeted training opportunities, in collaboration with Human Resources, is the next logical step. Sometimes the best training and development occurs within the job training, by way of redeploying people, based on project demands, in support of work requirements. I certainly recommend this viable training option remain a consideration.

2

CREATING A TALENT MANAGEMENT CULTURE

Moreover, in addition to accurately assessing whether current employees possess the required skills, talent management also enables leaders to "right size" their organization with a high degree of accuracy and fidelity. There is a fiduciary responsibility for every corporate CEO and every government senior executive to understand exactly why and where their recruitment and retention dollars are being applied across their respective organizations. One significant allocation is always related to the cost of the company's human resources—the cost of the current personnel. Senior leadership should be able to confidently align the skills of the workforce to the cost of the workforce to the products or services delivered by the workforce. Unfortunately, when provided this list of common questions, industry and government leaders admit they still struggle to accurately respond. As a reader, have you ever wondered or asked yourself the following talent management questions regarding your very own organization? In order to create a culture that applies and understands talent management, you could begin by querying your leadership, staff and teams and generating dialogue about talent management on a recurring and regular basis. The following questions can be used to enable, facilitate and guide a talent management discussion.

Questions:

1. How much did we spend last year on talent acquisition?
2. How much should we spend this year on talent acquisition?
3. How do we confirm we are making the highest priority talent acquisitions?
4. How integrated is our hiring efforts to our product lines and services?
5. How integrated is our training efforts to our product lines and services?
6. How much did we spend on training last year?
7. How much should we spend this year on training?
8. Did we make the best training investments?
9. Did we procure timely relevant training?
10. How to manage budgetary cuts that affect acquisition and training needs?

This is not a new management tool for incorporation into every manager's toolkit. However, some would contend talent management application has been slowly deployed across many organizations, making it still relatively new to today's environment, despite it being around since the 1970s. Why? You might ask.

The pursuit of answers by managers and leaders, based on investing in decisive fact-based information, is why talent management continues to be a current hot topic. Admitting, everything we do within and in support of our organizations involves people, so obtaining measurable data to make meaningful decisions is imperative.

If we're being honest, we acknowledge we have people working where they are not best suited because they simply do not possess the right skills at the right level of competence. Sometimes not only is it a struggle to ensure the timely execution of the project or a program, but it is a challenge for the employee trying to support the project or program. And from the employees' perspective, they may believe they possess the right leadership and technical skills at the right level of proficiency at the right time. Since the organization does not fully understand their skills' portfolio, it has, unfortunately, improperly misaligned them as a resource. When we employ all facets of talent management, to include the ability of each employee to fully understand his and her skill portfolio and what the required organizational skill demands are at each level while independently, assessing whether the employees possess the skills, the resultant data, insight, and findings become extremely valuable to any organization.

The ability to understand employed skills within an organization, required skills for performance and product delivery, and ultimately skill gaps at every level within each career field naturally brings organizations closer to closing skill gaps through targeted hiring, career development, and training. Talent management provides clear, data-driven insight into areas where employees lack required skills, allowing managers to determine whether it is a simple matter of sending employees to existing training, or whether the number of employees lacking this specific skill set warrants initiating discussions with Human Resources to invest in new, more relevant training.

By now you are probably wondering, with all the added value talent management brings, how you introduce talent management to your organization. The first step is to ensure you have a fact-based discussion with key stakeholders about the individual, managerial, and organizational gains of talent management; remember, talent management is about data-based decision making. I recommend you understand your organizational challenges, as it relates to talent, and confirm whether applying talent management will address the problems your organization is facing. One of your goals should be to avoid simply introducing another labor-intensive, burdensome tool to the workforce that is of little to no value. There is no doubt leaders mean well when they deploy new organizational tools, to include software products that address people related challenges. However, sometimes, through feedback, leaders of the organization learn their newly introduced tools do not solve the specific people related challenges, but instead bring about more work for its workforce. Typically, in these cases, all of the sunken costs and effort associated with attempting to address the challenges are viewed as inefficient and ineffective when meeting the organization's needs, and more importantly, it simply frustrates the workforce.

The way in which you approach creating a talent management culture, while introducing talent management, is by performing an organizational assessment and cost-benefit analysis prior to deciding to design and deploy a Talent management tool. This approach provides a better understanding and educates key stakeholders on the time and cost commitment required to ensure talent management success. This is critically based on a strong collaborative partnership that must be formed, and an initial investment of time and money required for the identification and development of the work, skills, training, and data/metric modules of a talent management tool. The information you gather during your organizational assessment and cost-benefit analysis phase will allow you to build political capital with influential leaders and identify those willing to partner, sponsor, and advocate your talent management efforts. I cannot overemphasize how important it is to have informed, supportive leaders in your organization, ones willing to have crucial conversations to remove all barriers at any level to ensure the successful deployment of the company's talent management initiatives. At a high level, the following ten talent management steps are recommended for a successful program implementation.

1. Identify leaders within your organization that understand the talent related challenges and whom will not only politically advocate for talent management but be willing to financially align and allocate resources toward a talent management program. Additionally, learn the talent management challenges other organizations faced and how they overcame them, so you are able to share success stories from other relatable organizations formerly faced with similar talent management challenges.

2. Socialize, early and continuously, the potential individual, managerial, and organizational talent management across the organization. Specifically, coordinate time at executive and supervisory meetings, workforce brown bag and lunch-and-learn training sessions, town hall discussions, and collective bargaining units and union meetings, to name a few, to discuss talent management and its benefits and progress. This approach will ensure you are educating the workforce, capturing any concerns they may have, and more importantly, addressing their needs by incorporating their requirements into your talent management processes and products. As a reminder, you want all workforce constituents vested in your talent management program from the start. Maximizing communication will increase interest and engagement.

3. Conduct necessary negotiations with key stakeholders and respective collective bargaining units or unions, which are influential groups in any organization. Consequently, you want to spend time building social and political capital with these entities. My discovery was the stakeholders and union representatives are truly about protecting the interest of the workforce Early conversations with bargaining units and unions proved invaluable; they quickly understand how talent

management would improve employee relations; enhance professional growth; and increase access and opportunities for their constituents.

4. Identify a team of representatives to lead the talent management initiative. Many employees support organization initiatives by assuming additional duties in concert with their official position requirements. However, supporting the establishment of a successful talent management program warrants some dedicated resources as with any major company project, in order to yield some quick wins and continue building momentum that result in longer lasting success. If you are to be successful, you will need a team of dedicated resources to support your efforts. Lastly, a corporation's decision to dedicate resources to any effort speaks to the organization's commitment of the project. A team of full-time resources, scaled to your organization's needs—but more importantly, dedicated to partner with workforce members to design and deploy talent management processes and tools—will ensure your organization's success.

5. Conduct an organizational assessment to understand people, their expectations and the products and services they deliver. In the 7 Habits of Highly Effective People, written by author Stephen Covey, he expresses how one must "seek first to understand, then to be understood," as Habit 5. This thought process extends beyond leadership and applies to talent management as well. Since talent management programs are customizable and scalable and designed to meet the unique needs of an organization in support of its business model, one must conduct an organizational assessment prior to considering a best-fit talent management solution. Specifically, there must be discussions with leaders and managers about their workforce

members' roles and responsibilities, so you capture what the leaders and managers believe are products of its team members. However, the richness of the organizational assessment is the direct communications with the workforce about their actual roles, responsibilities, and product delivery. This direct voice of the customer will enable you to design a grassroots talent management tool, centered on your most important resource: your talent! Companies, such as Talent and Technical Solutions, Inc., offer both commercial off the shelf talent management products and customizable, scalable talent management products. Sometimes modifying a commercial off the shelf talent management product, or customizing the best fit for your company is one of the best ways to ensure increase employee participation, improve employee engagement, and maximize utilization of your talent management tools.

6. Partner with technical subject matter experts (SMEs) to determine current and future work and skills demands, at the respective level of proficiency. The greatest return on investment (ROI) will be gained by the clarity resulting from your ability to understand and document current and future work, the anticipated deliverables, and the skills your organization will need to produce the deliverables and get the work accomplished. The format in which you choose to used capture the work and skills requirement will serve as the blueprint for your talent management tool design.

Current Work	Future Work	Technical Area	Product/ Service	Knowledge, Skills & Abilities	Proficiency Level
- Task... - Task... - Task...	- Task... - Task... - Task...	- Occupational Competency - Occupational Competency - Occupational Competency	- Engineering Investigation Report - Strategic Planning Document - Contract Performance Assessment	- Knowledge of Information Collection & Analysis - Skilled in Collaboration, Partnering, & Relationships - Ability to Process System Application, Assessment & Integration	- Advanced - Intermediate - Expert

7. Select technical subject matter experts to develop or identify what should comprise the talent management tool functionality and specifications, based on organizational assessment findings and voice of the customer feedback from the workforce. When you identify the dedicated resources to support your talent management program, although they may be the best to lead the talent management initiative, it is not likely they are going to be experts in all the needed technical areas. Consequently, a small cadre of technical leaders should augment the dedicated team, serving in an adjunct or advisory capacity. These leaders must be familiar with the workforce needs and organizational demands and be able to assist with influencing and shaping tool functionality and specifications.

8. Coordinate employees' career development and management discussions, and then assess the onboarding skill and proficiency

levels achieved in concert with the designed career progression roadmaps. Initially, employees assess their knowledge, skills and abilities (KSAs) and proficiency levels, based on identified focus areas, which aligned to the leadership and technical competencies of their position that complement their work requirements. The supervisor assessment occurs after each employee completes a self-assessment regarding his or her current skills and collaborates with the supervisor to compare and discuss the onboard skill assessment results versus the demanded skills of the position. As a result of the talent management assessment, an individualized and organizational data-based snapshot of resident talent confirms if the current employee meets the required level of leadership and technical competence needed to produce the products and services of the position. As an employee, the application of talent management principles cultivates learning, knowledge management, and career development, promoting individuals to take accountability and ownership of a more consistent, clearly defined career plan. Through the application of talent management principles, managers and leaders can simulate today's accessions and tomorrow's separations to determine the best workforce skills mix for desired organizational results. Skills assessments facilitate dialogue and often enable employees, for the first time, to better understand management's expectations and how to best align their capabilities to their positions to optimally perform at their very best. Additionally, these assessments allow each employee to review the required skills at the next highest level, enabling employees to determine if they possess the required skills to be promotable. Talent management skill assessments support employees' ability to communicate with data the whys for specific training. The results of an employee's skills assessment provides managers the ability to take a holistic view of training and experience. The dialogue that results allows the manager to effectively engage in a meaningful development conversation with employees, enabling the prioritization of training efforts and available rotational experiences. Moreover, for many employees and their supervisors, this will be a great moment of clarity and growth. The opportunity to have timely career development and management discussions with his or her supervisor, outside traditional performance cycles, is going to ignite the power within each employee to take accountability and ownership of his or her career. Widely populated career progression roadmaps will not only demystify success but will illustrate transparency, opening the door for all employees to have opportunity and access to grow and fairly compete for current and future positions. Career development and management discussions with employees and supervisors will result in targeted career discussions centered on where the employee stands and what his or her career aspirations are. In addition, the immeasurable trust from which an employee and supervisor must build their relationship flourishes from these recurring discussions. Oftentimes there is a fear on both sides—the employees and the supervisors—to speak freely and advise candidly when it comes to someone's career, unless there is a trusted professional relationship.

9. Perform data/gap analysis, and leverage talent management tool reports. In order to perform data/gap analysis, you must identify and understand the difference between the demanded skills and the skills you have on board across your talented workforce. One of your talent management tool features and functionalities

must be a portfolio of relevant and repeatable reports, for all levels of your workforce: the employees, managers, and leaders. In the design of your reports, you must learn what questions are being asked today by your most important resource, of your most important resource, and about your most important resource—your talent. I highly recommend you advertise developmental opportunities to assist with performing the tasks needed in this area. You have the information gained from the organizational assessment surveys and voice of the customer feedback in the development of your talent management reporting capability and capacity. Remember, every employee, at every level, plays a role in talent management, so be certain your collected data is meaningful and measurable. Your talent management reports are valuable because they are the solution to unanswered people-related questions asked repeatedly throughout the organization. For a moment, think about the change in organizational dynamic skill-gap assessments this talent management process would bring to the employee and manager. These assessments eliminate the need for an employee to convince his or her manager why allowing participation in specific training is a good investment. Leveraging the skills assessments, the employee and manager can change the conversation to a dialogue that is more valuable and focused on short- and long-term goal setting, resulting in impactful contributions at all levels.

10. Identify training, development, and risk mitigation strategies. Talent management principles one through three, specifically understanding your products and services; documenting required skills and experiences; and identifying the talent across the organization and performing gap analysis, add clarity to the organizations' work requirements, skills needed, and onboarding

skill gaps. However, principle four focuses mainly on identifying targeted training and development opportunities, while offering risk mitigation strategies to things that impede talent development and management. The contracted training courses or designed leadership and technical development programs are solely based on current and future identified gaps. No longer should we offer training focused on obsolete requirements. Furthermore, if the training is not germane to what work you perform today, or will be challenged to perform tomorrow, these training and development opportunities should no longer be offered. With the scarcity of training resources, companies must be intentional with how training dollars are spent. Hence, training resources must align to skill gaps to mitigate the risk to successfully deliver products and manage project execution. Another amazing unintentional consequence of deploying an effective talent management program is that your new insight into your entire employee portfolio of talent permits you to leverage the KSAs of your workforce, in other capacities, including knowledge transfer training opportunities such as internal brown bag and lunch-and-learn training sessions taught by your resident experts. This sharing of knowledge and information across the organization not only promotes synergy, creates collaborative opportunities, forms partnership, and increases connectedness but also results in cost avoidance and cost savings of training dollars.

For the first time in some organizations' history, they are discovering exactly why they are investing in specific training and what the expected result is for the employee upon completion, which is improved or increased performance.

3

ACHIEVING TALENT MANAGEMENT GOALS

Furthermore, now let us assume your organization is interested in the establishment and implementation of a talent management program, and you have confirmed there is organizational commitment, political support, and financial backing of the program. Allow me to be the first to say that you are well on your way to achieving your talent management goals.

Following is a checklist of helpful hints to help you identify your supportive talent management program attributes and characteristics.

1. To be most effective, pick a start date to officially launch your talent management program.

2. Only incorporate relevant technical and leadership training requirements that reduce the knowledge gap between what your workforce knows and what it needs to know.

3. Development of consistent procedures that are documented in the form of a user manual, which addresses the intent of the work and skills requirements, and provides guidance in determining the employees' level of proficiency. Additionally, in the event, there is a unique product or skill that needs to be addressed outside of the identified process, provisions to address

exceptions to the documented procedures, such as the capture of a unique skill, should be annotated and communicated upfront. Lastly, it is highly recommended this manual be complete and available prior to implementation.

4. Recommend employee and supervisor training be developed and conducted prior to implementation.

5. The establishment of a technically diverse governance board or multilevel employee steering committee is essential to confirm continuity and consistency, as well as assure the voice of the workforce remains represented during maintenance and sustainment phases.

6. The identification of a dedicated power team, inclusive of dedicated and adjunct workforce members, will guarantee your talent management program management success. Congratulations again. You are well on your way!

If talent management is implemented correctly, its deployment across the organization will promote a paradigm shift and a change in culture, eliminating employees' anxieties and concerns that being transparent regarding skill shortfalls have solely negative career impacts but conversely generate developmental opportunities that create career opportunities.

Talent Management Vignette: In a former talent management program manager position, I was responsible for providing people, processes, and technical knowledge necessary to conduct manpower and organizational analyses. My challenge as a key leader within a newly formed department was to establish an overarching process to identify and implement a comprehensive workforce planning (talent management) program, which would ultimately include one standard policy, process, and tool to capture and assess workforce skills, requirements, and gaps.

Responding to leadership and workforce concerns, I consulted with numerous internal and external entities, as well as synthesized local, national, and international policies to implement an innovative talent management program. In developing my strategy, I discarded several conventional alternatives: one included setting arbitrary workforce onboarding targets and attempting to achieve them, relying on staffing without critical thought related to skills. This was my opportunity to lead strategic change by taking intelligent, risk-based steps to identify and implement state-of-the-art/best-in-class practices.

Originally, the functionally diverse team comprised of technical SMEs (subject matter experts) was resistant to investing their efforts to change the existing broken process. However, my abilities related to change management practices prepared me to address the tensions and dissatisfaction with the current state. I remained adaptive, open to discussion, and encouraged ideas. Ultimately, my leadership, motivation, technical expertise, and strategic ability to lead change resulted in the implementation of a comprehensive talent management program. I led the team in adopting policies and practices of performing talent gap analysis, creating agile, adaptive methodologies to forecast skills gaps for individuals, and technical communities.

In addition to innovative leadership practices, I incorporated data from mathematical models to establish talent risk-assessment criteria to identify and measure severity levels related to skill gaps, both current and future, reflecting and predicting organizational health. This resulted in the design, development, and deployment of a revolutionary talent management process for approximately thirty-six thousand employees. I capitalized on existing information technology capabilities to represent a total workforce systems model, reducing multiple systems of recordkeeping while combining redundant functions and processes. I instituted transformational workforce management practices and processes across nine work sites representing eight technical communities.

Another leading change with talent management opportunity occurred during my career. My challenge was to develop a corporate document that demystified career progression, a longstanding workforce issue. Specifically, there was a perceived mystery surrounding the required skills to successfully progress within any career field. Career progression for one individual appeared to have no repeatable relevance when related to the career progression of another within the same technical community, leading to suspicion and frustration among the workforce.

Like some companies, this organization lacked a corporate document that identified the expected proficiencies required for individuals to progress, tailored to each level, within each technical community. In response, I built and shared an end-state vision, which served as a catalyst for organizational change and motivated a small cadre of knowledgeable workforce members to identify the skills required by each technical community at every level. Specifically, I provided people, processes, and technical knowledge necessary to conduct manpower and organizational analyses. My challenge as a key leader, within this newly formed department, was to establish an overarching process to identify and implement a comprehensive workforce planning (talent management) program, which would ultimately include one standard policy, process, and tool to capture and assess workforce skills, requirements and gaps. Additionally, the previously referenced diverse team, representing a small cadre of knowledgeable technical workforce members, from several work sites, also provided the technical components to the career guidebook and made it a success. A career guidebook is the direct result of collaboration and synergy across all leadership and technical competencies. Comprised of career roadmaps, it is intended to be a self-help tool to assist employees on their professional career journey. It is a unique product because it serves as a cornerstone for professional development and career planning. It can help identify the KSAs (knowledge, skills and abilities) needed to advance within our organization. Additionally, a career guidebook can assist with informing choices about career progression and serve as a tool for mentors advising individuals on required and suggested training, formal and informal developmental opportunities, and rotational career-enhancing assignments for consideration.

The career guidebook provided career progression paths for tens of thousands of workforce members; this was groundbreaking since specific skill identification approaches had never been collectively codified at the corporate level. I dealt effectively with pressure, and remained optimistic and persistent, even under adversity, which resulted in a career guidebook that allowed every workforce member, regardless of grade or technical community, to learn and understand his or her potential career progression.

Shortly after publishing the hard copy career guidebook, I realized paper documents were not cost effective or optimal for maintaining current content. Consequently, I delivered the first automated version of the career guidebook on a server, allowing it to receive well beyond thirty thousand unique user hits on its internal server in fewer than two years. This is one of the most impactful changes experienced across all nine of the company's sites.

Delivering talent management solutions results in cost avoidance and financial savings; enabling employees and supervisors to target training; the flexibility to compare and move employees and work between similar professional areas; and includes a targeted hiring strategy that aids strategic recruiting and hiring.

4

UNDERSTANDING ORGANIZATIONAL WORK DEMANDS

As many companies focus on recapitalizing, modernizing, and sustaining its technology, it is important to understand what products are being produced and at what rate based on the company's preferred business model. It is critical to have a thorough understanding of the work, its speed, its quality, and other factors in order to fully align to the organization's mission. Therefore, what is the meaning of "thorough understanding" of the work demands of your organization?

Specifically, today's organizational leaders must be able to evaluate work requirements; recognize trends resulting from a range of analytic policies, processes, and tools, on a number of differentiating data elements; and apply a variety of data mining and intelligence techniques to make adequate business decisions. Understanding obsolete work, anticipating current work, and predicting future work will confirm an organization is equipped to best manage its current and future skills.

Organizations attempt to understand their work demand and workforce requirements through a myriad of different methods; some utilize the easiest and most ineffective: counting employees by quarter, by fiscal year, by department and comparing the current year numbers to past years' numbers. This method yields the least valuable and actionable data.

Other organizations perform complex analyses, such as averaging trend analysis queries, and merging and comparing data from multitudes of sources. This often results in "paralysis by analysis," where leadership is unable to decipher meaning from the vast, multi-sourced quantities of information. In order for a preferred business model to prove progressive and profitable, there must be a clear understanding of the work and the necessary skills to support current and emergent business requirements. The priority of an organization must be to avoid losing critical workforce skills needed for periods of technological recapitalization, modernization, or sustainment, considering implications of workforce attrition and skills atrophy. Hence, based upon its priorities, the desired state for all organizations should be to clearly identify, qualify, and quantify its work to a level of understanding for its workforce.

The talent management approach to identifying work detects the requirement for skills at a certain level of proficiency. By now you are probably wondering how to best identify work requirements. As previously indicated, it is important to understand and document current and future work requirements and align talent management decisions to best manage and predict work and talent risk.

Now, allow me share the best approach to applying the first principle of talent management, understanding your organization's work.

First, an organization must decide where its talent management information will reside. For example, what tool will capture and store this information and generate the resulting data analytics? Consequently, it is imperative to identify a common tool structure, lexicon, and business rule to describe your current and future work products and services.

I highly recommend you document and disseminate your business rules, articulating the details regarding your talent management approach in the simplest, most relevant, repeatable, and relatable format. Understanding the business rules is critical to ensure accuracy and consistency of skill and work details. Remember, there must be clarity of the effort associated with producing each product and service. Individuals, managers, and leaders, at all levels of the organization, must have insight into the talent and work requirements to properly contribute to and balance risks. The results of the work requirements and skills identification are the integration of the work and skills framework—in this case, talent management principles one and two, which uniquely connect work requirements to skills requirements.

Provided here are a few talent management steps for your consideration:

1. Define the work requirements and skill requirements. Focused on meeting your organization's goals and objectives, define the work and corresponding level of effort to be performed. Anticipate and validate all the resources needed, including your number-one resource, people.

2. Develop a staffing plan based on available leadership and technical skills and corresponding proficiency levels by reviewing and discussing the skills needed to complete the defined work, and compare the needed skills to the onboarding skills available to support the defined work. To accurately identify this information, you must enlist subject matter experts (SMEs) representing each competency to provide the detailed KSAs for each career field at each level.

3. Ensure accuracy and fidelity of data analysis with continuous reviewing, monitoring, and capturing of feedback by performing data analytics to include workforce assessments.

4. Understand any and all risk factors and the implications through other areas of the business by identifying training and development opportunities and talent acquisition approaches to manage and mitigate risk.

A company can increase its performance and profit when it applies the principles of talent management to its workforce decision-making process. Many organizations recognize a need for a consistent, accessible means of measuring the health of their talent perspective as they move through periods of technological recapitalizing, modernizing, and sustaining. Preserving and maintaining a highly skilled, diverse, and flexible workforce is fundamental to any organization's ability to perform. In this work requirement phase of talent management, you cultivate an ability to capture the power of your workforce contributions in today's workload discussions. Furthermore, you identify and correlate the capabilities of your current workforce to the skills projected to be required to meet your organization's work requirement demands of the future. In addition, you gain in-depth understanding of the capability of your talented workforce to improve the way you approach and respond to your evolving work demands, which is critical to organizational success. The ability to normalize data to predict and prescribe work demand and its accompanying resources is a vantage point users of talent management embrace.

The need to enable a closed-looped workforce shaping framework, focused on talent management, identifies gaps between existing workforce capability and current and future work demand signal, provides rigor in baselining your workforce, and measures data to ensure your workforce's skill sets at every level align to required skills to efficiently and effectively provide the products or services of the organization.

Two important focuses of talent management is for every organization to improve its understanding of the work and the workforce with the objective of tying requirements of people, products, gaps, and training to a common closed-loop talent management framework. This aids organizations in understanding the implications of the external environment and influences internal processes (hiring, recruiting, training, workforce development, facilities utilization, resource management, among others). The result is a well-defined assessment of your organization's overall health, which provides you the ability to lead the workforce with confidence into the future environment of your respective industry.

Application of this talent management principle to understand your organization's work principles ensures organizations comprehend the work and skills of their total workforce and move closer toward an agile, flexible, capabilities-based approach to working. The good news is healthy business relationships are formed in the spirit of collaborative skill and work discussions, to identify with confidence the capabilities of the current workforce to produce the products or services and to determine the best methods to close skill gaps for the greater good of the organization. This principle ensures consistency, transparency, and visibility of work and required skills throughout the organization.

5

DOCUMENTING REQUIRED SKILLS AND EXPERIENCE

Here we focus on skills from the perspective of an employee and from a manager or leader. The perspective of the employee is essential, as this is where we all start when first hired: struggling to gain a full understanding of the position and its detailed description of duties and responsibilities. Even if I am selling life insurance, my ultimate product is a secured policy. Therefore, understanding the skills needed for the insurance-selling position and its broader impact on the insurance company is essential. Consequently, as an employee, it is important to learn how to become a contributing member of an organization by connecting to other people and appreciating the products you collaborate on and work to deliver.

Companies invest a significant amount of resources in hiring and training their workforce, specifically talent acquisition and talent development. However, how are companies assuring they are receiving the best return on investment (ROI) on their recruitment and retention dollars, as it relates to directly improving production and increasing profits? Companies confirm it is costing more to attract, recruit, and retain value-added talent. Many company managers expressed their frustrations with difficulties of attracting and retaining millennials, who will represent their future workforce, despite their significant talent acquisition and development investments. Although adults between the ages of 22 and 38 years old, also known as millennials, have an employment turnover rate that is trending downward; individuals between the ages of 6 and 24 years old, also known as Generation X, have a turnover rate that is still of growing concern, as companies begin to position themselves to welcome Generation X leaders into the workforce.

While talent development is important, it is equally important to appreciate how talent management increases employee engagement, which also improves retention. Reportedly, in October 2020, according to combining Gallup's measurements for 2020, 36% of employees are engaged. On any given day, in my opinion, this percentage is suboptimal. Ideally, we want 100% of employees fully engaged at all times.

Prior to addressing the documentation of required skills and experiences, let us assess your level of understanding of the second talent management principle, documenting required skills and experience, by performing a self-assessment health check before we dive in.

Self-Assessment Health Check

1. Do you understand the work requirements of your position and your organization?
2. Are you fully aware of your current technical and leadership proficiency levels, and how they compare to the demanded technical and leadership proficiency levels of your position?
3. Are you hiring today's talent for the challenges your organization will face tomorrow?
4. Can you discuss which skills are trending, in comparison to which skills are obsolete, within your organization?
5. Do you understand how talent is inventoried or managed within your company?

6. Do you know when to forgo talent acquisitions and instead retrain and utilize existing talent?

7. Can you confirm what your organization must do to ensure that the right talent and levels of proficiency continue to evolve?

8. Do you know what your overall workforce should look like from a skill-set perspective?

9. Are you aware of the availability of certain skills in your industry?

10. Can you validate your talent portfolio yields propositional value for your organization?

11. Do you know and apply the best methodologies to attract the needed talent for your organization in order to ensure a vantage point over your competitors?

12. Do you have knowledge of what talent trends in what market sectors your organization should be following?

13. Can you confirm if your workforce is engaged and fully employed throughout the organization? How can you be certain?

14. Are you able to discuss how your company meaningfully measures success?

15. Is it your belief that individuals own their careers within your organization, and are progressing and aligning to the mission of your company?

16. Is it your belief that individuals own their careers within your organization?

17. Do you know if people within your organization are struggling to confirm if their efforts align with their expected performance contributions?

18. Have you led any type of talent management initiative, on any scale, in which your workforce members were able to flourish by gaining expert understanding of current processes, identifying and socializing shortfalls, and diagnosing causes of key poor performance indicators?

19. How do you know, when people return from training, the invested training was required in order for them to perform in a manner that increases their organizational contributions?

20. Are you leveraging transformative technology to perform data mining and develop solutions that shape and influence the decisions of small and large diverse teams within your organization?

21. Do you capitalize on relational talent management data to improve velocity and felicity across your organizational product lines and services? If you have answered at least seventeen of the twenty-one assessment questions affirmatively, please pause to applaud your organization for their talent management efforts to date. In addition, if you answered fewer than fifteen of the twenty-one questions affirmatively, go easy on yourself, as you are just reading this book to join me on this talent management journey. These assessment questions are the basis of hard aspects of talent management that are often complicated, particularly if data is not readily available and consistently reviewed and applied to substantiate and engage in decision-making talent management discussions.

Typically, when employees attrite, we recruit. We address what is known as a staffing gap instead of closing what is recognized in the world of talent management as a skill gap. Honestly, this is another talent management principle activity that distinguishes it from human resources. These are simple concepts on the surface but a little more complicated to manage when you really dive deeper into understanding their organizational applicability. If you are applying true talent management, people in your organization, at all levels, understand their direct visible connections to the mission. Additionally, when you employ talent management, your workforce believe they represent the solutions, and their focus is achieving their progressive levels of proficiency to impact the changing and shaping of your organizational direction.

Supervisors, managers, and leaders should affirm to employees, with data, how their meaningful and measurable contributions directly affect the daily success of the organization.

Talent Management Vignette: For many years, I worked for an organization that made huge training investments, specifically focused on leadership and technical training development. Similar to many other organizations, the looming questions were always focused around whether we had accurately identified the necessary training, if the training was timely, and if the training investments would generate direct development and production improvement impacts. If so, how will our organization measure the development and production improvement impacts?

Consequently, which managerial measures should be in place if your organization is to assess whether its training investments generated positive development and production impacts?

It is now time we become clear and deliberate in how we gather talent management data to perform analytics to drive the organization, not just by fostering quantitative resource discussions but through qualitative resource discussions based on the performance of the talent within the organization.

Do you have access to valuable talent management data regarding your workforce members? Of course the idea is to have individual and organizational data that is not intrusive so workforce members view it as meaningful information to be shared with organizational leaders, used in a manner that benefits both the organization and individual employees.

Furthermore, let us lean in to the learning culture that results from talent management. The incorporation of talent management promotes a learning organization culture. In a learning environment, employees partner with internal and external customers; increasing flexibility, agility and adaptability; expanding their sphere of influence to engage and empower people in the interest of organizational success. Moreover, employees calculate talent value to program management success, to include people, product and service impact, and measures/metrics. Enhancing talent by fostering a learning organization environment accelerates productivity and processes innovation; it sustains it with continuous process improvement. In a learning organization culture, employees should believe they are a part of a team, one that operates with a collaborative and collective spirit to ensure the success of the organization's mission and vision. As leaders, it is my recommendation we make ourselves professionally transparent to ensure our organization's success.

Chapter 4 is a critical chapter because of the importance of understanding skills when it comes to appreciating the talent within your organization. Simply stated, people matter and must connect to the products they deliver while understanding the skills they need to perform optimally to deliver said products. Even if you are in the service industry, there is the expected delivery of a product, for which you contribute. Specifically, there is something you and others are accountable for delivering. Providing one's best performance occurs when an individual understands his or her organizational contributions.

The level of understanding I am referencing must go deeper than just the leadership level; it must take place at the individual levels of the organization, from new to seasoned employees.

Talent Management Vignette: Addressing the skill gap. Interestingly, I am typically nervous when I start any new position and am even more nervous when I am not clear about the skills needed to enhance my role and responsibilities to ensure I hit the ground running and am continuously performing optimally. Often, at a senior level, I am replacing another senior employee, so there are great expectations that I was hired with the right skills at the right time for the right position and should deliver immediate results. Additionally, there is a misbelief that as a senior person, by leaving one senior position to accept another, you already know everything you should know at the right level of granularity.

I find this misbelief very interesting—a common misunderstanding, I might add—because although you are filling a staffing gap, you may not be filling a skill gap right away, which is why talent management assessments are critical. Please understand that just because there is a staffing gap closure attempt, a skill gap, the difference between the skills needed for your position and the skills you have on board to effectively perform in the position could remain, at least for a period of time, until the access to the right leadership and development opportunities are afforded. The greater the gap means you are going to need to work harder to develop the identified skills needed for your position to mitigate programmatic risks to ensure expected optimal performance.

To assist with achieving management's expectations of me in a new position, I often ask myself, "How are my behavioral leadership skills in comparison to what I need to know for my position? Do I have the right behavioral, technical competencies? What behavioral leadership and technical competencies should I have in order to continue to be successful in my position? Am I competent at the right level of proficiency? Because this will also be a factor in the workload planning discussions, and product scheduling and delivery meetings, as it relates to the time it takes to deliver my performance products."

If you share pride in accountability and ownership, the ability to personally complete informal talent management assessments on yourself proves invaluable. The understanding of skills gaps is critical when making hiring decisions.

Hires and promotions typically happen one of two ways. A person is hired because he or she has proven performance or verifiable organizational contributions, either at the current organization or at a previously employed organization. Specifically, an employee has repeatedly performed, and based on that performance, hiring or advancements to other levels are imminent.

The second hiring and promotion approach occurs when an employee is hired or promoted based on his or her potential. In this approach, the employee typically lacks the required skills for the new position and has an identified and documented skill gap to close. However, there is a staunch belief among managers that this employee has the potential, and with the right resourcing, coaching, and mentoring, he or she will close the skill gaps over a reasonable amount of time with minimal programmatic impacts.

Allow me to dive a bit more into my thoughts, resulting from experience, regarding the potential versus performance perspective, as I am extremely passionate about this topic because it has intentional and unintentional consequences. It is extremely important for an organization's overall morale to hire and promote with a sense of honesty and integrity. One way to ring out biases and ensure there is honesty and integrity associated with your hiring and promotion practices is to institutionalize talent management assessments that drive talent acquisitions.

The utilization of talent management assessments allow leaders and managers to gain insight into the organization's entire workforce talent portfolio, which ensures the right people with the right talent are developing and afforded equal and fair access to advancement opportunities. The optic that honesty and integrity are not associated with the hiring and promotion practices of your organization demotivates top performers from contributing fully and negatively affects average employees from striving to increase their performance under the belief "the game is rigged." Furthermore, it will also encourage your top performers to seek other employment opportunities where they feel their individual contributions to the organization are recognized and rewarded with future advancement opportunities.

Now, let us further apply commonly used terms, such as KSAs (knowledge, skills and abilities). Knowledge is defined as one's level of understanding. For example, I may have read an article regarding systems analysis; however, it does not mean I actually know how to apply the needed analytical processes to perform systems analysis.

KSAs are categorized by five proficiency levels: Awareness, Basic General Knowledge, Intermediate General Knowledge, Advanced Detailed Knowledge and Expert In-Depth Knowledge. We can mature these proficiency levels over time through training and experience. Using the systems analysis example, the question is: if an employee has demonstrated skills in conducting systems analysis, how will you know? What will you measure? Skills can be developed, transferred, and redeployed, while abilities are repeatedly demonstrative. Specifically, although I have knowledge of systems analysis (the application of analytical processes to the planning, design, and implementation of new and improved information systems to meet a customer's business requirements), and I am skilled in conducting systems analysis, I must be able to conduct repeated systems analysis in order to demonstrate my abilities. The common integration of all three KSAs is critical to supporting talent management.

Below is a systems analysis example.

	Awareness	Basic General Knowledge	Intermediate General Knowledge	Advanced Detailed Knowledge	Expert In-Depth Knowledge
Competency Behaviors	- Knowledge of ... - Skilled in ... - Ability to measure and identify the effectiveness of Information Technology products and services to maximize the performance of related systems	- Knowledge of ... - Skilled in... - Ability to link discreet computing subsystems and software applications in order to deliver Information Technology services	- Knowledge of ... - Skilled in... - Ability to test and evaluate Information Technologies during development and acquisition to ensure internal and external requirements are met	- Knowledge of ... - Skilled in - Ability to develop strategy and plans for management of Information Technology resources in order to enable organizational missions	- Knowledge of ... - Skilled in ... - Ability to execute an Information Technology project from initiation to sustainment to fulfill established requirements that meet specified business missions
Recommended Training and/or Development	- Basic Systems Management - Organization Overview Training	- Software Management - Communication Training - Collaboration Course Training	- Fundamentals of Systems Management - Mid-Level Management Training	- Intermediate Information Systems - Emotional Intelligence Training	- Advanced Software Acquisition Management - Senior Leadership Development Training

There is an understanding when you are hired: that you bring a certain talent, inclusive of your KSAs, to the team. Your KSAs are obviously important and critical to its success, which is why the organization hired you. Even when the most senior leaders and managers move across organizations, branches, or divisions, there is a belief their skills are critical and transferable; however, these senior leaders and managers will also seek understanding of the job requirements to perform in their new roles. Asking ourselves if we have the right level of proficiency is something almost all of us silently ask, at some point, regardless of the positional authority we have within the organization.

My advice is to give yourself a break when you start a new position, and know your skills are transferable—likely very portable, I might add. Typically, it takes me a good six months to feel like, oh, these work products make sense, and I can be a major contributor in this new role, where I actually understand what I am now doing. Conversely, the first week or two, maybe even a month or two, I think, *Oh my goodness, what have I done to my career by accepting this position?* I am certain this is relatable, knowing a number of times people focus on transferring from position to position in search of the one that will elevate them to their next desired career level. I suggest you try not to focus on the positions but instead focus on the KSAs you have that are transferable and portable. More importantly, focus on the KSAs you gain in your new roles. This is critical. Do not be upset with yourself when you attend a meeting for your new position and it seems like everyone else is speaking in a different language, and you find yourself reaching for your cell phone to text a friend, in a panic to manage your anxiety and emotional intelligence. You are silently saying, "I was once on top of my game. There is no way I will ever understand this." The key is knowing what is required of you, understanding the KSAs that align to your respective position—specifically, what KSAs you bring to the position and the skill gaps in your new role.

As an employee reporting to work, you should expect to be and insist on being presented some sort of career progression roadmap that allows consideration of several trajectories and multiple career path opportunities. Specifically, if you are not presented with this roadmap, you should ask your immediate supervisor for one. This demonstrates you will be seeking ways in which to learn and mature in your career development. You could simply state, "I am coming into this new role in a new organization. Is there a career progression roadmap that illustrates what opportunities may be available to me at some point during my career? What leadership skills are critical to the success of the organization?"

You want to be able to see opportunities and growth within an organization, because you ideally want to work for an organization filled with possibilities. When you think of what your manager and leader know, think of their KSAs and their various levels of proficiency. Do not expect to advance your knowledge or become an expert overnight. The discovery of what you need to know, and the level in which you need to know it, is significant because you may not need to know everything at the level of granularity, particularly if you are leading other technical SMEs. Stated differently, you do not need to be an expert in every knowledge area linked to your position. Perhaps you simply need to be aware of particular knowledge areas, or only need to have some familiarity at the intermediate level of proficiency, instead of an expert or mastery level.

What is really going to be critical is knowing that in order to deliver the products and services of your organization, you must have a thorough understanding of the knowledge, skills and abilities (KSAs) that will enable you to optimally perform. There must be a clear understanding of the KSAs across all five levels of proficiency, Awareness, Basic General Knowledge, Intermediate General Knowledge, Advanced Detailed Knowledge and Expert In-Depth Knowledge, recognizing you do not have to be advanced or an expert in everything.

Also, if you are a midlevel manager, be certain you convey to your employees that it is acceptable to possess varying levels of proficiency in different technical and leadership areas. From a managerial perspective, sitting with an employee and outlining their specific organizational products and service contributions, highlighting the KSAs germane to their position, recognizing the employee for having some skills and the abilities to mature into the needed level of mastery, and acknowledging the transferred KSAs is all a part of the talent management process. Additionally, a positive supervisor-employee relationship is a great way to partner to support an organization, while illustrating transparency and building trust for your talent management approach.

Applying the principles of talent management does not negate or diffuse the role of supervisors, leaders, and mentors. Actually, talent management does the opposite: it strengthens the employee-supervisor relationship and enables a framed, facilitated conversation regarding an employee's career development and management. In addition, talent management alleviates the challenge for supervisors to recollect the scope of what is shared with every employee in their organization when having one-on-one career development and management conversations.

The consistency in a supervisor's approach to developing people and career management messaging alleviates the inevitable optics of favored employees, or "plum projects" assigned to certain preferred personnel. There should also be electronic or hard copy versions of the talent management results, made available to individuals and managers, as it solidifies the jointly established talent management partnership.

Supervisors reinforce what is required and has been demonstrated by employees, in comparison to and contrast with how employees believe they are performing. The commitment of a supervisor, leader, manager, or mentor should be to enable the success of the employees for the betterment of the organization, with a collaborative spirit.

I am passionate about the role of supervisors. Many organizations undermine their impact or significance, but supervisors play a critical role, as they are the heart of a workforce. Often, organizations analyze a significant amount of data to make workforce-related decisions. The role of a supervisor is key to the analytic results, and of utmost importance to how the workforce feels about the organizational data and its use.

Supervisors are the first line of defense of any company. An employee's decision to remain with a company is often directly influenced by the relationship with his or her supervisor. Frankly, I have spent more time with my direct supervisors than other senior leaders within any of the organizations I supported. My best supervisors were the ones who honestly and openly partnered with me to influence and guide my career choices, outside of the performance cycle. My favorite supervisors enabled and empowered me to guide and manage my career accordingly.

My positive supervisory relationship experiences improved my organizational connectivity and overall performance. From an employee's perspective, it is extremely important for you, as their supervisor, to invest your time forming a relationship with them. Supervisors determine whom they recommend for leadership development programs, the priority of which deliverables or products are going to be due, and by whom. Supervisors also determine which employee interfaces with the highest leaders of an organization; affording access and opportunity to certain employees plays an extremely crucial role.

The best supervisors apply consistent and fair processes to advising, coaching, guiding, mentoring, and teaching all their employees to meet their individual needs as they align with the overarching organizational demands. A good supervisory relationship is important because professional work challenges can spill over into our personal lives, making things complicated. A strong relationship between the supervisor and employee supports the work/life balance we all seek, allowing thoughts outside work to be spent on non-work-related topics. The continuous improvement invested in leadership and technical KSAs will enable you to progress in your career. Additionally, you will be relieved to discover you already possess some of the KSAs required for the position, which is why you were hired. The reality is some of your KSAs are germane to your position, which is why it is key to document all your KSAs as they relate to the job requirements and your deliverables. Furthermore, when you have a leadership or technical proficiency gap, become comfortable asking others who are in the position to help you close those gaps.

You must learn to be comfortable highlighting your areas of needed improvement because it is acceptable to continue learning while in any position. Over time, you will become more proficient with the increased understanding of your position. The richness of talent management is identifying exactly what you need to learn and how it relates to your improving your performance.

I hope that after communicating what talent management is and how it can be used in your organization, you are asking, "How do I get started?" Great! The crux of talent management resides in defining the expected KSAs for each position at each level. For example, immediately hired after graduating from college, what required KSAs is an engineer supposed to have upon entry into the organization? After identifying each required proficiency, define those required at the next higher level. This process of required KSAs covers entry position to the highest engineering position, where the KSAs most likely reflect more significant managerial capabilities. The SMEs from each career field must be responsible for this critical information.

Work Requirements based on Organizational Products and Service models	Skills Needed to Optimally Perform the Work Requirement	Position Determination, based on Work Requirements and Skills Demand	Skills Assessment of Individual hired into the Position	Gap Analysis between Skills Needed to Perform and resident Skills of the Position holder	Training and Development increasing Proficiency Levels

This definition of the required KSAs for every position, for every career field is the foundation of talent management implementation. I am being completely transparent when I share that this is a significant time investment for your organization. These KSAs are also referred to as behavior competencies, defined as a measurable pattern of knowledge, skills, abilities, behaviors, and other characteristics that an individual needs in order to successfully perform work roles or occupational functions.

The five levels of proficiency are awareness, basic, intermediate, expert, and advanced. Behavior competencies, knowledge, skills and abilities, are clearly defined areas of proficiency.

Awareness—Employee has gained basic knowledge and can assist others on a limited basis. It is important to note that attending training does not automatically mean a proficiency level will increase. Instead, the experience of applying new skills develops proficiency levels.

Basic (general knowledge)—Employee can address most standard problems, is competent at day-to-day application of skills, and is able to present concepts, information, and solutions. The employee will use a variety of development activities to increase experience and proficiency level (for example, reading manuals and on-the-job training).

Intermediate (general knowledge)—Employee can resolve difficult problems, is competent at day-to-day application of skills, and is able to develop concepts, analyze information, and propose solutions. The employee will demonstrate understanding of concepts and processes with occasional guidance.

Advanced (detailed knowledge)—Employee at this level is able to provide solutions for unusual or nonstandard problems and issues, is aware of alternative options and approaches to situations, can guide or advise others, and is able to look ahead and predict. At this level, employees are capable and confident in applying their skills in ordinary and unusual situations. They may be involved in coaching or mentoring activities.

Expert (detailed knowledge)—Employee is seen as setting an example for others, is a recognized expert and visionary in the field, provides guidance to others in the application of their skills to related areas, shows advanced thinking, develops innovative approaches, and stretches others' thinking and challenges them to excel.

In summary, the five distinct proficiency levels will aid in understanding the capabilities of the workforce and better align it with the agency's mission, current needs, and future work requirements. The levels of proficiencies are intended to reflect an individual's depth of expertise in a leadership or technical competency or skill. Employees, managers, professional communities, functional offices, and leadership will apply these levels to locate expertise in a reliable and systematic manner. The levels will also be used in the employee development process to assist employees, managers, human resource employees, and talent management program managers to identify gaps and proficiency targets and provide opportunities to refine or enhance the individual's level of expertise in a selected area, while making talent management decisions in the best interest of the organization. Skill documentation, workforce alignment, and skill gap identification and mitigation is talent management simplistically defined.

6

PERFORMING GAP ASSESSMENTS AND ANALYSIS

Managing energy and time in all aspects of your life, including your work life, is empowering. For this reason, time spent in training classes should increase your professional value in your organization. Ideally, the more you know, the more indispensable you are to your organization. Frankly, I am a life learner. I enjoy development and training and have taken an endless amount of leadership development and training courses over the many years of being in work environments. I find it interesting when an instructor asks a student why he or she is here, meaning what would be the desired takeaway from the class experience. I absolutely love the question, because I believe we should ask ourselves about everything in which we are applying energy and time.

So why are you where you are right now? I guess I should have asked this question at the beginning of the book. For example, why are you reading this book? What attracted you to it? Are you struggling in certain talent management areas? Sometimes there are people, including senior managers and leaders, who do not appreciate attending the classes because they are extremely busy and deem many classes of lesser value in comparison to their other outstanding day-to-day tasking.

Training and development should be approached with intention and purpose. When registering for training, your focus should be on targeting a knowledge, skill, or ability—something you are lacking or need to improve. It is not cost effective for any organization to invest dollars in training its workforce in courses that are not germane to how the employees will increase performance for the good of the organization. Why attend a training class that does not close a gap when you can intentionally spend time attending a training class with purpose?

Sometimes employees attend classes because they were informed it was a good experience or perhaps an easy class, or they attended at the advice of a supervisor or colleague, without assurance that it would close a gap and improve performance.

Talent management includes targeted learning that builds performance at all levels. Organizations simply must eliminate all aspects of wastefulness, including resources spent on training and development that does not close skills gaps of required proficiencies. There is no time for employees to waste sitting in classes when it takes them away from working the products they are hired to produce. As an individual, talent management is about progressing in your career to deliver optimal performance results that allow you to have an impact on your organization.

If you are taking training classes that are not related to the products you produce or do not close a particular skill gap at your level of proficiency, attending said classes may be considered wasteful. As we shift our paradigm to be deliberate about our approach to training, not only will we view training differently, our organizations will value training investments differently. Ideally, when you return from a training class, there should be a difference in your performance as a direct result.

The training you invest in should also coincide with achieving your long-term career goals. As you assess your current job and look to the future, it is important to lay out your individual career goals. The term individual is important. Each of us have different strengths, different aspirations, and different available opportunities.

In thinking about these individual goals, I offer the following focus areas for your consideration. The first focus should be on making a meaningful contribution to your organization. Whatever is your organization's mission, you should definitely strive to align your career efforts and contributions toward it. Although you may have started your career for other reasons, being impactful at your organization is hopefully a primary reason for continuing your focus on career progression. If you are a manager or leader, one of your responsibilities is to assist the people on your team to identify what they need to progress in their careers. Another focus should be on attaining proficiency in your chosen field. This is where the offering of a career guidebook or roadmap can be useful.

Each functional area should have itemized traits (behavioral characteristics) and training course recommendations for each level of proficiency, from awareness to expert. A certain level of proficiency is desired for every employee, but not everyone will become an expert-in-depth technical professional, nor do they need to in order to be successful. Although some may forge toward advancing technical mastery, others will gravitate toward supervisory positions where exposure to multiple technical career fields is the desired outcome. For example, a business budget financial manager might want to attain some proficiency in cost estimation, earn value management, and other diverse financial management training to have a breadth and depth of related financial experience.

The bottom line is some professionals will look for opportunities to reinvent themselves and move into an unrelated field where there is increased demand from the organization or industry, while others will remain in their field and become the experts that make them technical leaders in their professional discipline. In support of any organization, you should dedicate yourself to training and development for the good of the organization and achievement of your career goals.

Prior to requesting any training course, develop a list of your strengths and areas for improvement. Set a notional timeline for attainment of proficiency in areas that meet your short- and long-term goals while giving consideration to how you can contribute to your organization's mission. Hold yourself accountable for monitoring your progress in closing the skill gaps you identified and the achievement of your short-term goals.

7

ENABLING DEVELOPMENT AND MANAGEMENT RESOURCES

One of talent management's greatest assets is its automated approach to providing better visibility into the collective leadership and technical proficiency levels of the workforce. Managers can conduct multiple resource planning scenarios to effectively and efficiently satisfy current and future organizational needs. Talent management offers a wide array of organizational gains and benefits to leaders, managers, and individuals, including the ability to baseline its employees' Knowledge, Skills and Abilities (KSAs) within specific focus areas and measure those outcomes against the work requirement to determine gaps, identify the severity of skill gaps for any required skill, and target the necessary training requirements to close the skill gaps.

Talent management also provides individualized and organizational databased snapshots of resident talent and identifies if the current employee is capable of producing products and services required of the position. The application of talent management principles cultivate learning, knowledge management, and career development, promoting individuals to take accountability and ownership of a more consistent, clearly defined career plan. Through the application of talent management principles, managers and leaders can simulate today's accessions and tomorrow's separations to determine the best workforce mix for desired organizational results. Adopting the higher/broader level of talent management, as a future approach to identifying skills and ultimately cross training them within a talent management tool will assist your organization with its data-collection ability.

When you share information regarding talent management, are you confident that you are able to discuss this data with the highest degree of accuracy and fidelity? Interpretation of existing data outside a talent management tool will lack accuracy and fidelity, resulting from inconsistencies of data capture. Consequently, a blueprint of work requirements to coding in a talent management tool will be necessary to provide consistent talent reporting. Please note a talent management tool goes beyond numerically capturing staffing gaps and includes the identification of work requirements and addresses skill levels in an acceptable level of proficiency.

The talent management tool needs to capture current and future work requirements, as well as needed training. Gap analysis should be completed to understand where the leadership and technical competencies of today's workforce reside, in comparison to where tomorrow's leadership and technical competence should be in regards to skills. A well-designed talent management tool enables preparation, anticipation, and formation of a workforce in the best possible position to meet the work requirements.

Developing a skills module in your talent management tool provides the necessary formation and architecture to collect and measure gaps in the workforce. In order to collect and measure them, you must consistently identify the work requirements and crosswalk them to tasks performed by each workforce member. The workload assessment should also assign the proficiency needed for each task. You must ensure all organizational units use this same talent management model, as their baseline of information, to ensure consistency by tracking work efforts and yielding consistent reports.

The training module of the talent management tool should leverage the compilation of data resulting from employee assessments, supervisory assessments, and customer feedback surveys to collect training data on employees and determine varying training requirements.

When a company decides to fully invest in institutionalized talent management, it moves towards a capabilities-based approach of doing business and understands the skills of the total workforce is a critical step to meeting the organization's objectives. Technical communities are challenged with meeting this objective because oftentimes there is no consistent or standard policy, process, or tool to apply when determining leadership and technical skills requirements. Consequently, it is difficult to thoroughly assess skill gap areas, accurately predict talent resources, and mitigate potential program and personnel risk. Your dedicated talent management team will develop a standardized talent management framework to define current skills with the Subject Matter Experts (SMEs) and identify future skill requirements.

Whether you decide to organically design your tool or procure a customizable talent management solution from an industry partner, the overall objective is to provide a standardized talent management framework that will enhance your organization's ability to consistently identify and assess skill gap areas, accurately manage and predict required talent resources, and mitigate potential program and personnel risks.

Establish a standard skills framework that includes

1. Common workforce skills taxonomy and definitions to provide an aggregated capability;
2. Identification of work products and services;

3. Clarity of work functions in each skill area;

4. Standard methods to identify skills required by the work functions;

5. Normalization of an approach to identify skill gaps;

6. Assurance that the agreed-to standardized skills identification process links to people, work functions, skills, products and processes, requirement demands, and learning opportunities; and

7. Confirmation that skills framework captures data/information required to produce metrics that identify current and future skill requirements and gaps.

When determining whether you should organically design your talent management solution or procure a customizable talent management tool from an industry partner, consider the talent management tool requirements approach listed below. Then decide if the internal development or external acquisition will meet your organization's immediate and long-term talent management demands.

A skills capability census must be conducted to inventory existing tools or methods that are currently used by your organization to capture skills. The common methods, across companies, for documenting skills are standalone databases, spreadsheets, and random documents. Data and information collected through these methods align closely with the functional descriptions and approved organizational structures. However, a more logical option that serves as a better basis to categorize skills in a framework is to link people and their skills to products and services. The proposed actions are as follows:

1. Develop a skills framework that comprises a three-tier work/ skill area taxonomy and considers your organizational construct

o   Tier 1: Functional Area—Grouping of activities or processes based on their need in accomplishing one or more tasks, in support of product and service delivery

o   Tier 2: Core Capability—Unique ability that an organization develops that cannot be easily imitated

o   Tier 3: Specialty Area—A division of experience, activity, or knowledge

2. Develop Work Functions for Each Specialty Area

o   Work functions may be positions within each specialty area

o   Develop KSAs required for each work function

Measures of Success Tied to Talent

Challenges

Let us discuss a few challenges you will need to address if this is your first attempt at designing and developing a talent management tool. Communication of methodology from the top down will be critical for success. Implementation requires top-level management/ leadership support and mandate to maximize employee engagement and participation. Not having both may result in inconsistency for employees, minimized return on investment of the talent management tool, and undermining of your talent management efforts.

If you have employees associated with collective bargaining units or unions across your organization, I recommend negotiating with these respective groups prior to a talent management tool implementation in order to avoid deployment delays. Additionally, if you can, invite collective bargaining units or unions into your talent management tool design discussions.

The skills identification effort could warrant a sizable investment of time (such as identifying work and skills). Emergent workload requirements, in addition to existing heavy day-to-day workload, must all be documented. Consequently, it is important to ensure the information in your talent management tool remains current. If possible, identify a skills coach or talent management program manager to assist with the skill identification efforts, particularly as the process evolves.

Identification of a governance board or steering group committee to continue to solicit feedback, and evaluate and monitor your talent management tool, to ensure it is relevant and relatable is very important.

Communication and negotiation with technical leaders of your organization regarding the work and the staffing must occur to ensure consistency within the tool. Agreement of the work task and skills crosswalk amongst the technical community will also prove beneficial. Keep in mind, most technical leaders are largely understaffed and overworked, assigned full time to assist with their teams and manage other technical matters. So, perhaps a dedicated tiger team (generally, specialists assembled to work on a certain goal or solve a particular problem) to assist with the tool requirements or specifications will likely be required to be successful in your talent management tool design. Changes in implementation and interviews with employees could require specific changes that might not necessarily be applicable or desired across your entire organization; consequently, some talent management tool governance is warranted. It is extremely important to over communicate how talent management will not replace human resources; instead, talent management is complementary to human resources in that it enables verifiable, fact-based decision making. The need to make this connection is important to alleviate any political conflict that could result from a lack of understanding of how these two technical groups should best perform to ensure the successful competitive dominance of their organization. Your talent management and human resource organizations must be seen as groups that cooperate with each other and operate from a place of collaboration in order to be efficient and effective.

Benefits

I would be remiss if I did not summarize the amazing benefits associated with designing and deploying a talent management tool. Skills identification helps define the career development path for employees, thereby improving morale. Skill identification allows consistency in training and a better understanding of skill requirements for employees, supervisors, managers, and leaders. It becomes a 360-degree measuring tool for KSAs that manifest into individual development plans for employees.

Skills identification and gap analysis provide employees and managers the ability to report qualitative/quantitative data and metrics to higher-level leaders and align to your organization's human capital or human resource initiatives and strategies.

Understanding the tasks for new employees and knowledge and experiences needed to perform tasks and advance, in one central tool, will inspire and motivate employees to learn at their own pace and expectations and work standards across the workforce.

Your talent management tool will provide continuous analysis of workforce skills and eliminate reactively shaping the workforce to meet the business mission. The process places emphasis on planning, which ultimately saves the organization time and money while improving performance and increasing profits.

Lastly, the identification of skills and gaps provide a means to assess attrition and support retention efforts.

Risks

In the spirit of transparency, allow me to share a few risk factors. The most important is that without management/leadership support, there may be inconsistent implementation of your attempt at deploying a talent management tool.

The limited availability of personnel with sufficient skills to develop and maintain your talent management tool could place the success of subject efforts at risk. Your current organization initiatives already in process will likely compete with a heavy day-to-day workload. As a result, consider soliciting contract support services for this effort. I can assure you the return on your company investment will yield great dividends.

As skills are communicated with employees, changes may be necessary. Leadership needs to address how these changes will be incorporated from an organizational perspective. Advocacy and support, at all levels, could be challenging based on the results of the implementation and voice of the customer feedback from managers and employees. The commitment of all employees will be necessary to ensure continuity of intent, movement forward, and other factors.

A potential exists for the skills to be used in a manner other than that originally intended. Employees may perceive the skills identification is associated with performance, in lieu of career development and management. It could also create some unintentional stress within the workforce for those who feel they are at one proficiency level, but discover through evaluation they require proficiency at a different level, resulting in possible performance issues and decreased morale.

Interestingly, my experience has been the total opposite. More than 99 percent of the employees are assessed at a higher proficiency level than the employees anticipated. Consequently, the skills assessment exceeded the employees' expectation and improved their morale, in regard to the tasks they performed.

For the first time, the employees were receiving positive feedback outside their performance cycle that enabled them to take ownership and improve their product delivery. Another risk factor is if an employee has many years in the workforce, performing work tasks a certain way and doing it very well, the skills identification process could require he or she attend new training identified to meet a specific proficiency level. The training for such an experienced individual could be considered an inefficient use of time. Some employees may limit learning experiences to those specified in the skills at their required proficiency levels. Unfortunately, attainment of proficiency levels may be misconstrued by employees, and could create a false expectation of automatic promotions. Consequently, comprehensive employee socialization of the talent management program goals will contribute to the further expansion of employees' professional development.

In addition to working with your employees, it is important to ensure you address the following talent management considerations that may become a topic of discussion as you move forward with soliciting advocacy and support for your best fit talent management solution:

1. Multiple evaluators across the organization with a lack of thorough understanding of the organization's talent management program could make it difficult to measure employee equitably.
2. Skills measured still contain a bit of subjectivity. Technical skills and proficiency levels are considered hard skills. Conversely, it is the employees' self-initiative and ability to apply that technical knowledge that makes them a good subject matter expert (SME), which may include the application of soft skills.

3. Availability of funding and resources required for initial investment and sustainment to identify work, conduct surveys, identify work, describe and define talent management tool/systems requirement and modifications, conduct interviews, travel, and other factors. Employing some contractor support service experts to augment your workforce is a great risk mitigation strategy.

4. The turnover of team membership, supervisors and managers can cause deployment delays and follow-up difficulties.

5. Process sustainment could be impacted, because of an already heavy employee workload, other initiatives, and emergent work requirements. Consequently, a dedicated governance board or steering committee is critical to your talent management program success.

6. I would like to offer that many programs and projects sometimes do not succeed because of a lack of feedback and follow through over time.

7. Success demands leadership advocacy and direction, management oversight and enforcement, and organization follow through and feedback.

Lessons Learned

Moreover, I want to discuss a few lessons learned, based on my years of experience.

1. Even within an organization, different tools and systems houses talent management data that may be of value.

2. The talent management team membership must be consistent, as these individuals will need to have access to key stakeholders and insight into all impacting data systems.

3. Over communicate, with clarity and consistency, the purpose and goals of the talent management tool.

4. Ensure your talent management team is inclusive of some SMEs, whom will ultimately serve as key players when implementing your talent management tool.

5. Leverage small groups of technical workforce members to identify skills. This approach will reduce time required for skills identification and approvals.

6. Partner to research and define the best gap analysis metrics for your environment. Consider what is used by other companies, government agencies and nonprofit organizations.

8

DISCUSSING MENTORSHIP AND ITS ORGANIZATIONAL VALUE

Mentoring is a developmental relationship that partners an experienced person (mentor) with a less experienced person (protégé). The role of the mentor is to guide the professional development of the protégé. By sharing the knowledge and insights learned through years of experience and organizational perspectives, the mentor candidly offers the protégé, within the context of mutual respect and trust, insight and guidance to do the job more effectively or for career progress. Furthermore, mentoring provides the opportunity for the protégé to further enhance his or her skills and knowledge while attaining developmental goals.

The benefits impact the mentor and protégé. For the mentor, it sharpens management, leadership, and interpersonal skills, expands the professional network, and increases personal and professional satisfaction. For the protégé, mentoring increases learning, personal and professional growth, assists with career planning, and expands professional networks.

Mentoring is also a risk mitigation strategy for closing a talent management skills gap. There are six common types, and the following outlines each one.

1. **Traditional Mentoring**—This pairs a senior workforce member with a junior workforce member. This top-down model may be the most effective way to create a mentoring culture and cultivate skills and knowledge throughout an organization.

2. **Group Mentoring**—Group mentoring requires a mentor to work with several mentees at one time. The group meets routinely to discuss various topics. Combining senior and peer mentoring, the mentor and the peers assist one another learn and develop appropriate skills and knowledge.

3. **Short-Term, Goal-Oriented Mentoring**—Focuses on specific goals for a set time limit.

4. **Peer-to-Peer Mentoring**—Pairs employees with similar skill sets with each other.

5. **Speed Mentoring**—Time-limited meetings where a mentee meets with several mentors focusing on quick-hit information and networking.

6. **Reverse Mentoring**—Provides the opportunity for senior executives to become the mentees with junior workforce members becoming the mentors. It is used to offer senior members the opportunity to learn about the organization from the employee's perspective.

The benefits of mentoring have positive impacts for both the mentor and protégé.

Mentoring will enable you to

1. clarify career goals and identify strengths and weaknesses;
2. gain visibility/demonstrate your capabilities;
3. share candid information about the organization;
4. engage in smart risk-taking;
5. test ideas and plans with a trusted sounding board;

6. share insight into opportunities to overcome professional shortfalls in confidential setting;

7. propose professional solutions, based on personal experiences, to workplace challenges and issues;

8. increase organizational awareness and information;

9. improve self-esteem and confidence when dealing with professionals;

10. achieve new goals and explore alternatives with confidence;

11. handle a realistic perspective of the workplace;

12. increase knowledge of workplace dos and don'ts;

13. receive advice on career development and progression;

14. renew enthusiasm;

15. receive encouragement and support on an individual basis;

16. gain insight into potential opportunities; and

17. expand networks that include senior level professionals.

As a protégé, you must have an active, engaging role in your mentor and protégé relationship, in order to maximize your opportunity of experiencing the previously shared benefits.

Let us further identify a few steps you, the protégé, should consider to proactively strengthen your mentoring relationship:

1. identify initial goals and objectives;

2. use those goals and objectives to help determine the professional skills and personal attributes of a potential mentor;

3. seek and initiate communication with potential mentors;

4. communicate expectations for the relationship;

5. allocate time and energy;

6. stay receptive to feedback and coaching and committed to self-improvement;

7. keep commitments and renegotiate appropriately;

8. consider development and execution of a partnership plan;

9. demonstrate willingness to assume responsibility for growth and development; and

10. raise issues of concern regarding career development.

Another important requirement of a protégé is the selection of a mentor. I recommend you consider performing the following:

1. be persistent in your quest for a mentor;

2. develop three goals you desire to achieve from the mentoring relationship;

3. select several prospective mentors for interviews before you request one;

4. create meaningful interview questions for your mentor;

5. schedule initial mentoring meeting session;

6. get acquainted by sharing your professional journey;

    o   have a resume available upon request

7. embrace authenticity and vulnerability during your mentoring meetings;

8. share some personal information (hobbies, interests);

9. discuss your short- and long-term goals and objectives;

10. pay attention, be intentional, be deliberate, be thoughtful;

11. show appreciation for your mentor's time, knowing every interaction is time consuming; and

12. notify and thank all prospective mentors after interview sessions.

As you prepare to meet with your mentor, I recommend you consider the following attributes and characteristics of a mentor:

1. refreshing, positive view of organization and individuals;

2. connects to large, professional networks;

3. is patient, tolerant, candid, and resourceful;
4. has the ability and desire to encourage;
5. understands the big picture;
6. generates useful suggestions;
7. schedules availability for ease of meeting coordinating;
8. is trustworthy, ethical, and nonjudgmental when you share the good, the bad, and the ugly;
9. skills in your current technical field or future field of interest; and
10. has active listening and probing, questioning skills, and confidence (in themselves and you).

Once you are selected as a mentor, set the mentoring relationship, to include setting the expectations for some of the following factors:

1. have reasonable expectations;
2. be an organization resource;
3. data is your friend;
4. provide constructive feedback;
5. allocate time and energy;
6. help the mentee achieve the goals he or she originally provided for the relationship;
7. follow through on commitments and renegotiate evolving mentor relationship appropriately;
8. establish expectations for the relationship;
9. embrace cultural differences, and consider enhancing your skills through cross-cultural communications courses;
10. counsel and advise cautiously;
11. be forthcoming and willing to share your knowledge and experience;
12. make a commitment and follow through;
13. ask questions about work and life experiences; and

14. recommend a regular meeting time and place.

The impact of having a mentor or becoming a mentor can have a tremendous effect on career and goal achievement. If your organization does not have a formal mentoring program, challenge yourself to follow the aforementioned guidance provided to find your mentor within the organization.

Lastly, of most importance, as a protégé, you should always ensure you go above and beyond to deliver assignments. You are the one person who can determine your career success. Healthy mentoring relationships will prove to be invaluable as you travel along your career journey. Your performance will create opportunities for you to move across your career field.

However, your relationships will generate opportunities for you to ascend within your career field. Specifically, your relationships will generate mobility by getting you noticed, paid, and potentially promoted. Just remember, if no one knows who you are, then no one can ever assist you with your career, or even one day serve as an advocate or sponsor for you.

9

APPLYING TALENT MANAGEMENT IN TODAY'S ENVIRONMENT

This chapter includes several interview responses that offer real-life talent management experiences from professionals who understand the four talent management principles: understanding work demands; documented required skills; assessing available skills and performing gap analysis, and the rich organizational gains promotion of application of these principles can yield. These professionals shared stories are enlightening and further inspire and motivate you to fully embrace and welcome talent management into your organization.

When asked what talent management means to you, the following responses were provided.

"I view talent management as one of the most impactful "tools" I have ever encountered. Throughout my career, I have experienced numerous new innovative tools that were promised to finally give the organization a shared data repository, eliminated redundant data calls, flexible methods for reporting, etc. never once has one delivered to its full promise.

While talent management provides several significant benefits to an organization, the most personally impressive are the numerous impacts directly derived from the self-assessments. For the first time in my professional history, employees are provided an objective list of required skills, tailored to their career field, on which to analyze their own current capabilities. The results of this assessment allow the individual to rate themselves, determine what skills they need acquire to progress; identify what training will close their skills gaps; and understand the correlation between possession of these skills to promotions and selection into career enhancing development programs.

The direct organizational benefits are also tremendous, utilizing this data to: steer the investment in training courses offered—critical from both a financial and investment perspective, aid in the selection of employees for promotion and participation in competitive professional development programs and alter the dreaded employee reviews to eliminate the subjectivity—allowing meaning dialogue, based on the employees own assessment, regarding training and career goals. Talent management minimizes the workforce's distrust in the degree of favoritism and subjectivity—transparent data available for all."

—Ms. Michele DeMoss-Coward
Naval Air Systems Command Logistics Director,
Workforce, Acquisition and Development (retired)

"The words talent management mean to me to plan, organize, staff, control, and direct a diverse and inclusive workforce, with the right skill sets, in the right place to achieve the desired organizational goals, objectives, and outcomes."

—Mr. Edward (Kurt) Threat
Acquisition Group Director,
Fleet Readiness Center Southwest

"As you well know, there are as many opinions of what talent management means as there are people. Everyone seems to see it a little differently, which is part of the problem. In my opinion, talent management is transforming into what could also be called human capital management. That said, talent management includes the elements of human capital management that address employees at all points in their respective careers, from recruitment to retirement.

The first part of talent management is strategic human capital planning, identifying those elements of the personnel required to manage and execute processes that enable employees. Other elements include hiring and retention; performance management; learning (not the same as training) and motivation, including employee engagement; compensation, including incentives and other forms of acknowledge; career development, including providing the professional development tools employees need to advance their careers; and succession planning."

—Ms. Pamela Jamieson
Jamieson Consulting Services

"Talent management means to me the organization or categorization of human capital. Specifically, when an organization seeks certain skill sets, titles and/or experiences for the purpose of executing identified tasks or assignments."

—Ms. Amy Purnell
Financial Business Analyst,
Federal Government

"Excitement, enthusiasm, employee engagement, recruitment, retention. Hiring the right people for the right position at the right time. Placing those people in a role where they can thrive not only for themselves but for the organization as well."

—Mr. Michael Taylor
Talent & Technical Solutions, COO

"Talent management represents the ability to ensure an organization is utilizing the talent brought by all members of the workforce. Many times this isn't the case because the employer doesn't know the knowledge, skills and abilities their employees bring to the table."

—Ms. Emily Harman
Department of the Navy,
Office of Small Business Programs Director (retired)

During a discussion regarding how employees currently apply talent management, or how they previously applied talent management to their organizations, talent management advocates shared the following experiences.

"I apply talent management on a daily basis by leveraging relationships based on professional and personal connections. For example, if tasked with an action that I may be unfamiliar with, I purposely seek assistance from someone who a) has experience with that tasker or b) someone I have a work relationship with who can assist or connect me with someone who can. Throughout my career, I started building my own talent management pool consisting of diverse professionals with whom I share a personal and/or professional connection. I consider this form of talent management an organic soft skill that is highly desirable yet overlooked by many."

—Ms. Amy Purnell
Financial Business Analyst,
Federal Government

"Teaching the employees industry's best practices. Assess our employees and examine where there is a niche. We develop their natural strengths and place them in a place where they are successful."

—Mr. Michael Taylor
Talent & Technical Solutions, COO

"I apply talent management within my organization by enlisting different perspectives to achieve the desired goals, objectives, and outcomes that my organization would like to produce. I rely on my diverse and inclusive workforce to define and evaluate problems to generate solutions and alternatives, so that I can make decisions to achieve the desired organizational goals, objectives and outcomes. The goodness in this approach is that I avoid blind spots, and I created a culture within my organization that promotes employee straight talk so that safe problem solving can occur."

—Mr. Edward (Kurt) Threat
Acquisition Group Director,
Fleet Readiness Center Southwest

"I applied talent management when I was the director of the Department of the Navy's Office of Small Business Programs. Typically, hiring managers weren't aware of the knowledge, skills and abilities required of small business professionals and made hiring decisions based on outdated standards."

—Ms. Emily Harman
Department of the Navy,
Office of Small Business Programs Director (retired)

During talent management interviews, experienced talent management benefactors shared what positive impacts the application of talent management had (or is still having) on their organization.

"After 100 percent implementation in my logistics area, with other parts of the organization closely completing implementation, talent management was halted. This was not based on any failure of talent management or its reception by the workforce. This was the direct result of Human resources recognizing they would no longer be the determining factor for every workforce-related and training-related decision.

This is a worthy cautionary inclusion to the talent management story—the very real political dynamics of talent management implementation. Historically, Human resources "owns" the entire workforce, training, hiring, and professional development arena. Talent management relegates Human Resources to more of a "recipient" versus lead role. The decisions regarding training, promotion, hiring, and professional development are based upon the talent management data and provided to Human Resources, with organizational leadership directing the Human Resources response. If your organization's Human resources has significant political sway, odds are they will not "go quietly" into this new role."

—Ms. Michele DeMoss-Coward
Naval Air Systems Command Logistics Director,
Workforce, Acquisition and Development (retired)

"Some elements of talent management are more effectively applied than others. For example, there are effective tools used in some federal government organizations to identify workforce skills and skills gaps as well as tools that provide searchable databases to identify employees across an organization who have skills, including leadership skills, for particular positions. The identification of skills, training requirements, and employees who possess those skills and have completed required training provide a strong candidate pool for open positions. Again, though, statutory and regulatory requirements prevent the federal government from legally selecting people for promotions and/or opportunities without applicable competition processes."

—Ms. Pamela Jamieson
Jamieson Consulting Services

"Talent management is more than matching a skill with a role or position. It is also about talent utilization, and identifying your passion. Not only can this person do the job, but they also love what they are doing. When you find people who enjoy what they do well, the impact is highly successful."

—Ms. Amy Purnell
Financial Business Analyst,
Federal Government

"The most positive impacts I see is employee retention. At my place of work we treat employees with dignity and respect. We treat them as professionals. This treatment plays a strong role with employee retention. We also find out where the employees talent resides.

We give them a sense of autonomy and place them where they like to work. We listen attentively to our employees and develop them with the latest tools and skills."

—Mr. Michael Taylor
Talent & Technical Solutions, COO

"As the director of the Department of the Navy's Office of Small Business Programs, I led a successful effort to develop a list of the knowledge, skills and abilities needed for small business professionals at different levels of the organization. We incorporated the final product into a small business professional career guidebook and established a rotational excellence program. These two significant efforts enabled exposed more people across the Department of the Navy to the role of small business professionals resulting in significant competition among highly qualified candidates for small business professional positions, and ultimately improved service to our customers."

—Ms. Emily Harman
Department of the Navy,
Office of Small Business Programs Director (retired)

"Successful application of talent management in my organization include creating a positive employee talent management culture, employee development, employee engagement, employee growth, employee recruitment and retention, and organizational vertical and horizontal alignment, to name a few positive impacts."

—Mr. Edward (Kurt) Threat
Acquisition Group Director,
Fleet Readiness Center Southwest

Talent management followers answered the question of how they advanced in their careers, and whether it was because of their organizations embracing talent management. If yes, describe how. If not, explain why.

"My response is yes and no. No, in the traditional association of the word "advanced"; I did not promote based upon my successful efforts leading implementation. However, if you would widen the definition of advanced, then … absolutely. I "advanced" in the eyes of leadership as I led the logistics team across the headquarters and sites through the entire process. I garnered recognition from all facets of the organization as a subject matter expert. I advanced in my knowledge, skills and abilities (KSAs) resident in my professional portfolio for participating from the initial meeting to fully successful implementation."

—Ms. Michele DeMoss-Coward
Naval Air Systems Command Logistics Director,
Workforce, Acquisition and Development (retired)

"No. I believe I advanced in my career because I made strategic decisions about my career roadmap. I competed for leadership development programs, lateral and promotion positions, and accepted rotational opportunities that no one else would take. My experience is broad, including program management, logistics, and human capital management. When I tried to return to program management after moving into the human capital management arena, I found roadblocks. There was little appreciation for my broad range of leadership and technical experience; rather, I was told that I made a decision when I moved out of a program manager position and couldn't return. I tried to make the case for the wealth of experience I gained in those other areas that would only make me a better program manager. This example shows a gross lack of embrace of talent management, even though the organization was developing a robust talent management tool and was working hard to convince leadership to adopt talent management practices. The words of support for the system did not match practice. Probably the most effective thing I did to advance my career was to have senior-level mentors who advised me and opened doors that might have never been opened. This was not a result of an organized talent management system; it was a matter of advising an employee who then took that advice and acted on it, taking chances and accepting positions that were uncomfortable but provided growth."

—Ms. Pamela Jamieson
Jamieson Consulting Services

"No, I do not. It has been my experience that most organizations do not hire someone until there is a need. By this time, you have now compromised the talent to fulfill the need. The hiring manager is not necessarily seeking the best talented for the position, he or she is seeking the best qualified based on their experiences.

Having the most experience does not always equate to being the best talented for a position."

—Ms. Amy Purnell
Financial Business Analyst,
Federal Government

"I advanced in my career because I took control of my career. In my previous organization, I did not see an effort by my leadership to develop me. So I took my career in my own hands and became proactive in educating myself, developing myself, gaining access to mentors, networking, and finally making a switch in career and my geographical location."

—Mr. Michael Taylor
Talent & Technical Solutions, COO

"No. It wasn't used as I was moving up. My organization did not benefit from all of my skills. People were lateraled into positions, and the reasons for the personnel moves weren't made clear. This resulted in a lot of mistrust throughout the organization and lack of employee engagement."

—Ms. Emily Harman
Department of the Navy,
Office of Small Business Programs (retired)

"Whole heartedly yes! My senior executive and her staff identified, developed, engaged, retained, and deployed me into an organizational make or break position to achieve the desired organizational goals, objectives, and outcomes."

—Mr. Edward (Kurt) Threat
Acquisition Group Director,
Fleet Readiness Center Southwest

When asked how they see companies or organizations benefiting from talent management in the future, various government, industry and nonprofit leaders responded as follows:

"The benefits in my first response did not include all the benefits associated with talent management. However, those are critical and need to be recognized. As talent management continues to be implemented, I am confident its greatest impacts will occur additional positive impacts will be identified when talent management is commonplace and expected to be relied upon by leadership and the workforce as the basis for numerous decisions in organizations.

For the workforce: imagine the impact of efficiencies reaped when employees "track" their progression of acquiring the required KSAs—no supervisor has to tell them what skills are required or share their subjective perspective. Employees understand what they skills they need to possess to promote and compete for professional development opportunities. They only request training to fill a recognized skills gap. This eliminates the "professional training groupies"—those that find multitudes of reasons to attend every possible training course. The evaluation process changes to become a discussion based upon a shared set of data: both the supervisor and employee discussing the skills and skills gaps and how to close them. Debate and confrontation is minimized as the discussion really is about, "What have you done to date to close your skills gaps?" "What have you contributed aligned to your position?" and "What are your plans for the next quarter?" disciplinary action related to performance is also based upon objective, organization-wide shared data. The mistrust regarding the influence of subjectivity connected to evaluations, training and development are significantly minimized. Employees can see the career roadmap for their field and determine with a clear set of criteria how far they desire to climb the ladder and what it takes to achieve the next step.

For the organization: the efficiencies and effectiveness of talent management in the future is somewhat limitless. Struggling to correlate the costs to the rationale for the number of employees, growth, impact of departures, and training investments—to name a few examples—are substantially reduced, if they exist at all. The political "fights" to grow departments or invest in training, select employees for promotion and opportunities are removed from the discussions, as shared data is the basis. The endless discussions at the leadership level attempting to align training courses to actual relevance no longer occur.

Clearly, the thousands (hundreds of thousands? millions?) of dollars invested in training programs becomes laser-focused on closing resident skills gaps. Once those gaps are sufficiently closed, leadership identifies, through data, the next skills gaps or "skills growth" for training. Promotions and competitive professional development selections have data-driven support. Recruitment is fact-based on closing organizational skills gaps or hiring for skills growth.

Evaluations are assessment-based and minimize unsuccessful employee/supervisor discussions. The hours saved at a combined organizational level are tremendous, which is critical because time is money."

—Ms. Michele DeMoss-Coward
Naval Air Systems Command Logistics Director,
Workforce, Acquisition and Development (retired)

"Until talent management practices become a part of the organization's culture, it will not be fully realized as an effective way of doing business. Tools that help the organization execute elements of talent management are good, but they do not enable the full benefits of talent management.

Talent management needs to be a primary component of an organization's human capital strategic planning. It should be the framework upon which the strategy is developed. Once that happens and it is implemented throughout all elements—thus becoming part of the culture, then talent management will be effective. Business as usual will never enable the innovation of talent management. Fitting the components of talent management into current practices and calling it talent management will not enable effective talent management.

Talent management needs to be seen as a 'system,' a group of interacting and interrelated elements that form a unified whole. This system is surrounded and influenced by its environment, its culture, and expressed by its functionality.

Again, it goes back to changing the culture of an organization so that the system can be enabled and effective."

—Ms. Pamela Jamieson
Jamieson Consulting Services

"It is my opinion that companies benefit more from talent management when they outsource this area. This reduces nepotism, racial profiling and other hidden basis, all preferences that could skew talent management data if conducted from within."

— Ms. Amy Purnell
Financial Business Analyst,
Federal Government

"I see companies not just placing bodies in positions. I see companies filling specific roles with people who have the skill sets and desire to work in that role."

—Mr. Michael Taylor
Talent & Technical Solutions, COO

"I think companies that use talent management will rise to the top in their field. This will take some time but with a well-implemented talent management system, companies will see employee engagement increase and turnover will decrease because employees will feel valued and trust leadership."

—Ms. Emily Harman
Department of the Navy,
Office of Small Business Programs Director (retired)

"In today's environment, organizations need talented people. Talented people, their ideas, and their intellectual capital provide a competitive advantage. Talent management is critical as talented people are a scare resource."

—Mr. Edward (Kurt) Threat
Acquisition Group Director,
Fleet Readiness Center Southwest

INTERVIEW TAKEAWAYS

In his talent management interview, Mr. Kurt Threat, Fleet readiness Center Southwest's Acquisition Group director, expresses the favorable impact of talent management in his organization is that it "includes creating a positive employee talent management culture that focuses on employee development, employee engagement, employee growth, employee recruitment and retention, and organizational vertical and horizontal alignment."

Ms. Pamela Jamieson, CEO of Jamieson Consulting Services, says such a powerful statement in her talent management interview, as she states, "When we face organizational limitations, it means we have to take all those elements that comprise talent management and force them into a model of fairness and equality."

I appreciate Ms. Amy Purnell, a Financial Business Analyst for the Federal Government, sharing "Talent management is more than matching a skill with a role or position. It is also about talent utilization, and identifying your passion."

Another good comment was offered by Mr. Michael Taylor, Talent and Technical Solutions Corporation, COO, when he indicates with talent management, "We (employers) give them (employees) a sense of autonomy and place them where they like to work."

In her talent management interview, Ms. Emily Harman, Department of the Navy Office of Small Business Programs Director, (retired), discusses how, "People were lateraled into positions and the reasons for the personnel moves weren't made clear. This resulted in a lot of mistrust throughout the organization and lack of employee engagement," which is a common occurrence when there is a lack of talent management.

Lastly, profoundly Ms. Michele DeMoss-Coward, Naval Air Systems Command Logistics Director Workforce, Acquisition and Development (retired), emphasizes, "Imagine the impact of efficiencies reaped when employees 'track' their progression." I want to leave you with this transformative statement...just imagine the individual, managerial and organizational progression that you will gain with the application and understanding of talent management.

In closing, I want to thank each interviewee, most sincerely, for taking the time to allow me to interview you for this book. I truly appreciate your willingness to share your talent management knowledge and experiences. Also, I am confident your insight and perspectives will enable individuals to expand their position and organizations to reach their talent management goals and objectives.

10

CONCLUSION

I am hopeful you have enjoyed our talent management journey together, and more importantly, you have learned some new talent management processes and practices you can immediately apply to expeditiously move your organization forward. I would like to summarize the ideal talent management product, as you continue to decide how you want to approach talent management, to include if you should organically design your talent management solution or procure these services from an industry expert.

Your talent management solution should infuse a best-fit strategy, manage changes associated with your dynamic business, and improve your current operations as needed. The goal is to gain understanding of the dynamics of your organization by performing observations, and identifying strengths and weaknesses, as well as determining a best-fit strategy to support your long-range workforce vision. These tasks are done by conducting surveys, interviews, and small focus groups with identified organizational SMEs.

Based on work demands and required skills, collaborate with your identified functional technical community leads to identify the KSAs across at least five levels of proficiency (awareness, basic, intermediate, expert, and advance) that best align to the work. Companies like

Talent and Technical Solutions, a leading talent management firm, are extremely proficient with validating behavioral leadership and technical competencies across the varying functional technical communities, ensuring the alignment of demanded work products to skills needed and offering analytic solutions. This provides understanding of the organizational work products and skills needed to deliver said work products and services.

In this phase of capturing behavioral leadership and technical competencies within your organization, you will highlight the skills you have onboard, germane (or not germane) to the delivery of your products while gaining insight into the current passion and future interest of your personnel. Each employee must complete a self-assessment using the identified leadership and technical competencies and proficiency levels, provided and validated by your SMEs. Direct supervisors will need to complete assessments of each employees, specifically what the employee knows verses what they should know. I highly recommend employees invite their peers, mentors, and others to also complete an assessment on their behalf, allowing them to receive 360-degree feedback. This will solidify your talent management approach.

The talent management model should increase employee engagement and enable a web-based skills gap and access analysis system to conduct multisource assessments for individuals, departments, leadership and technical competencies, and functional communities. Transparency into targeted training and isolated skill gaps is a natural byproduct from the talent management process, in addition to individual development plans. Talent management application will ease agility and promote validity, as skill requirements shift and work demands change.

Your talent management solution should provide your organization an in-depth understanding of

a. work in demand;

b. skills required for work;

c. existing skills on board; and

d. training demand.

Now you can guide your talent management decision-making process based on factual, verifiable data. In addition, you actually have talent management creditably codified throughout your organization. In this manner, you will be able to provide linkages between requirements your organization delivers, and identify skills you have, skills you need to redeploy and skills you need to recruit (a demand for human resources talent acquisition efforts).

Furthermore, talent management solutions should provide a holistic integrated talent management approach, which lends itself to many learning management and career development models, and creates standard and customized reports based on your organizational needs. Your talent management approach should allow for skill density health assessments and metrics by gathering information from employees and management that is useful for all stakeholders, driving decision making in a strategic way.

Moreover, this methodology will allow for targeted recruitment, targeted training, and targeted development needs. In addition, your talent management solution should consider performance measures, trends, and lag times, from gap assessment mapping and organizational assessments, data mining, and statistical analysis. When accurately applied your analysis will include individual, managerial and organizational predictive analysis and forecasted findings. You will also be able to create virtual team building, and access workload acceptance implications. The holistic talent management approach will answer the question if the human capital infrastructure in place will enable better decision-making about your most important resource… your talent! Furthermore, a holistic approach will provide all data we necessary to make fact-based decisions, take performance success measures and leverage multiple complimentary tools depending on what the needs are for the organization. Talent management will allow you to develop data collection instruments and structured databases that conduct basic analyses, and interprets data and draws conclusions and recommendations from findings for organizational decision making.

In closing, know your organizational challenges; take a bleak look at the effects of not being able to answer the questions throughout this book with a high degree of accuracy, confidence, and fidelity. In addition, if your company is struggling with talent acquisition (hiring) or talent retention (training and development), this can be another indicator there is a talent management problem worth further exploring. It is important to create a talent management model that leverages your current budgeted human capital management investments, in order to create a dynamic, high performing, diverse workforce that optimally executes to meet its mission needs and objectives. The best and brightest talent remains in high demand, while aging skills are becoming obsolete due to technological advances.

With talent management, your organization may still acquire the leadership and technical skills you need. You are likely competing for certain skills in high demand, so answering these questions with a high degree of fidelity, will ensure you acquire the best talent for your organization. I am confident your talent management efforts will continue to address the talent management challenges your organization is facing today by providing optimal talent management solutions that will guide your tomorrow.

If you are in need of additional talent management information or assistance, I would be delighted to continue to work with you by guiding you through the talent management process and sharing the fastest way to leverage your company's talent to build profits by building strong performance. So, please contact me by visiting my website (somervilleconsultinggroup.com) to complete the talent management profile, and receive a complimentary one-on-one thirty-minute session. I look forward to working with you.

With that said, congratulations! May you continue to enjoy your talent management journey as much as I have, because the finish is so worth it!

ABOUT THE AUTHOR

Entrepreneur and CEO Adrienne Somerville leads two companies, Somerville Consulting Group, LLC, and Talent and Technical Solutions, Inc. She graduated from Norfolk State University and Florida Institute of Technology, and received Executive business certifications from both Georgetown and Harvard University.

She has been a civil service leader, reservist, mentor, coach, speaker, philanthropist, and author. Additionally, she is the mother of two children.

Somerville is well known in the talent management field at the federal and state levels as well as many private organizations and businesses. Her technical knowledge and leadership skills are unmatched. Here Somerville shares her professional experience and extensive knowledge about talent management so you and your organization can enjoy the lessons learned and apply these principles to further enable you to achieve your desired level of success.